JIM
K·E·L·L·Y

by Bruce Weber

SCHOLASTIC INC.

New York • Toronto • London • Auckland • Sydney

Sᴘᴏʀᴛs Sʜᴏᴛs were conceived by Alan and Marc Boyko.

ISBN 0-590-46250-4

Copyright © 1992 by Scholastic Inc.
All rights reserved. Published by Scholastic Inc.

12 11 10 9 8 7 6 5 4 3 2 1   2 3 4 5 6 7/9

Printed in the U.S.A.   10
First Scholastic printing, October 1992

CONTENTS

On cold days in Buffalo, Kelly uses an official Bills muff to keep his hands warm.

CHAPTER ONE
GROWING UP

The town is beginning to disappear now. Hard times have chased many businesses out of business. The Chevy dealer went broke. So did the jewelry store, the liquor store, and the dime store. But in East Brady, Pennsylvania, there's still a winning spirit that's fueled by Jimmy Kelly, the former high school quarterback who has gone on to bigger and better things.

James Edward Kelly, the fourth of six brothers, was born in Pittsburgh on

Valentine's Day, February 14, 1960.

The competition in the Super Bowl is tough, but it doesn't compare to the competition in the Kelly household. The brothers were always competing at something. There was football in the large side yard, boxing anywhere, and rough stuff anytime.

"I feel badly about it now," says Jim. "My brothers and I fought all the time. We drove my mother crazy. I can remember that we made her cry. We were never in real trouble, but we were always getting into scrapes. Looking back, the six of us can't believe the things we did to our poor mother. She certainly had a tough enough job raising the six of us."

While their mother, Alice, was trying to deal with Jim and his brothers, their father, Joe, was trying to earn enough

Just like a downfield pass, a handoff must be accurate, too. Here Jim displays perfect form.

money to keep a roof over their heads and food on the table. That wasn't easy, either.

"My father had to work two jobs, sometimes three," remembers Jim. "The guy was terrific. But sometimes that wasn't enough. Times were tough. If he was laid off from work, it was a real struggle. I wasn't really old enough to understand, but I do remember having to go to bed after having only a piece of bread for dinner. But we stuck together, and we still stick together. There isn't a family that's any closer than ours."

The Kellys were an athletic family. Brother Pat wound up playing in the NFL (Baltimore and Detroit) and the World Football League (Birmingham). Brother Ray played for the University of Richmond, and brother Ed played for Slippery Rock.

But it quickly became apparent that young Jim might well be the best of the bunch. When he was 10, he was a national semifinalist in the famous NFL Punt, Pass, and Kick contest. There's a special photo in the Kelly home, where young Jim, in a bulky uniform, is getting an autographed football from one of his heroes, Pittsburgh Steelers quarterback Terry Bradshaw. Jim Kelly's dreams of football superstardom may well have begun that day.

The tough towns of western Pennsylvania have always been the breeding ground for amazing quarterbacks. George Blanda, Johnny Unitas, and Joe Namath, each a Hall-of-Famer, started out in the area. As did Dan Marino and Joe Montana. So it isn't surprising that the area should produce another superstar, Jim Kelly.

If his golf stroke were as accurate as his throwing arm, Jim could turn pro right away.

CHAPTER TWO

HIGH SCHOOL

The East Brady Bulldogs now belong to the history books. In 1990 the East Brady football team, led by a sophomore quarterback who broke Jim Kelly's single-season passing records, went 9–0. It was the last gasp for a school that had only 95 boys in the top three grades. No football-playing public school in Pennsylvania had fewer. By 1991 East Brady had closed, and the students were all shipped to Armstrong Central High School. All that was left of East Brady High School were the memories, many fueled by young Jim Kelly.

The 1975, '76, and '77 seasons were the glory days at East Brady. The hardworking men from the coal mine, the oil refinery, and the rubber plant would crowd around the football field at East Brady to watch Jim Kelly and his buddies play football. And did they play!

For three seasons, East Brady was almost unbeatable. The Bulldogs were 6–3 in Jim's sophomore year and would not lose again while Jim was in school. They improved to 9–0–1 during his junior year and to a perfect 10–0 in his senior season.

The 6'3" Kelly, weighing in at nearly 200 pounds, blew away Bulldog opponents with his rifle arm. In high school, he threw for 3,915 yards and 44 touchdowns, though he rarely passed during the second half of many games because the Bulldogs were usually so far ahead. The powerful Kelly was a force on defense, too. His size and athletic ability made him a premier linebacker. When the votes were counted, it surprised no one that Kelly was voted all-state at quarterback.

Jim's high school coach, Terry Henry, remembers: "We always knew Jim was special. By the time he made the varsity in the tenth grade, he'd already starred in our midget and junior high school programs.

"He played both ways, offense and defense, all the time. I tried to keep him out of the way on defense, but it was impossible. First, I put him at defensive end. Then I shifted him to linebacker. As a senior, he played safety. But he always had to be where the football was. He made all-conference as a defensive player, and he was our punter, too. But the key was his leadership. The other players always looked up to Jim, and he always delivered. In his final game, against Brockway, we needed to hold on to the ball to salt away the victory. Jim led the team down the field for 60 yards and a touchdown. He was magical."

To this day, Kelly pays tribute to his high school coach. At Super Bowl time, the coach is always there as Kelly's guest, even if the Bills aren't playing.

When the football season ended, Kelly just switched uniforms. A big banger on the basketball backboards, Jim starred for the East Brady hoop team. During his senior year, he led the Bulldogs to the state semifinals. He averaged 23 points and 20 rebounds per game. For East Brady's athletic depart-

An intense quarterback checks the opposing defense before getting the play under way.

ment, Kelly was a one-man wrecking crew.

But Jim doesn't think of it that way. He knows that team success requires team effort. "We all did it together," he says. And he means it. In addition to his old coach, several of his high school teammates are still among his closest friends.

By the time his senior season ended, Kelly's reputation had spread far beyond the outskirts of East Brady — beyond the borders of Pennsylvania, in fact. Dozens of college recruiters came calling, but Kelly had long before decided that Penn State, with its legendary coach, Joe Paterno, was his college of choice.

Trouble was, while Kelly was dreaming about becoming the Nittany Lions quarterback, Paterno was thinking linebacker. So when Kelly got the Penn State invitation, he said, "Thanks, but no thanks."

Jim finally said yes to the University of Miami (Florida) Hurricanes and their coach, Lou Saban. Miami had fallen on hard times and turned to Saban, the former coach of the Buffalo Bills and Denver Broncos, to turn the program around. That mission, Saban knew, would require a first-rate quarterback. "I had heard lots about Jim," said Saban. "He was a great leader, was extremely tough, and he had a great arm. I knew he was our guy." And so, in the fall of 1978, Jim Kelly became a Miami Hurricane.

In the huddle (and in the no-huddle, too), every Bill knows exactly who's in charge.

CHAPTER THREE

COLLEGE
—DAYS—

When Jim arrived in Miami, Lou Saban was gone. An opportunity for Saban to coach the Army team at West Point had been too good to turn down. His successor at Miami was Howard Schnellenberger, who had enjoyed a superb coaching career in the NFL. Superstar QBs Bert Jones and Bob Griese had been among his students.

"I hadn't recruited Kelly," says Schnellenberger. "I didn't know what he could do."

Jim sat out the 1978 season, a "redshirt year" in college sports talk. You go to school, you practice, but you don't play. But you still have four more years of eligibility to play.

A football freshman in 1979, Jim spent most of the early season watching from the sidelines. But when he got his chance against the Syracuse Orangemen, he jumped at it.

The Orangemen, led by Art Monk and Joe Morris, two future Super Bowl heroes, were loaded. By halftime, they had buried Miami. So Schnellenberger turned to his freshman quarterback, Kelly, and said, "Let's see what you can do."

Jim responded. He completed seven of 17 passes for 130 yards and even tossed a TD pass in the second half. More important, he kept the Hurricanes in the game. Miami had found a new quarterback.

The following Saturday, Kelly was the starter against—you guessed it—Penn State. As always, the Nittany Lions were among the nation's top teams. But with Jim at the controls, Miami pulled off one of the season's major upsets. He completed 18 of 30 passes for 280 yards and three TDs as Miami won, 26–10. Kelly's career was in gear, and the 'Canes were on their way back.

In Kelly's sophomore season, Miami finished its year in the Peach Bowl, with a 20–10 victory over Virginia Tech. It was the Hurricanes' first bowl appearance in 13 years.

Jim's junior year was even better. He completed 168 of 286 passes for 2,403 yards and 14 TDs. Three times he was chosen as the offensive player of the game on ABC-TV games-of-the-week. One of these games was a 17–14 victory over Penn State, then the No. 1 team in the nation. Though a couple of losses left Miami with a 9–2 season mark, the 'Canes had come back from the football dead, with Kelly in the driver's seat.

When Jim's senior season began, dreams of a Heisman Trophy were being dreamt all over Miami, but it wasn't to be. Jim suffered a shoulder separation in the season's third game, against Virginia Tech. His college career screeched to a halt, but he had shown the pro football world that he was the real thing. He wound up with 406 completions in 646 attempts (62.8%) and 32 touchdowns in his college career. He set new Miami records that were later broken by his successors, Bernie Kosar and Vinny Testaverde.

For the NFL, the quarterback class of 1983 was the richest in years. At draft time, six were snapped up in the first round, including top pick John Elway of Stanford, Tony Eason of Illinois, Dan Marino of Pitt, Todd Blackledge of Penn State, Ken O'Brien of California-Davis, and Jim Kelly of Miami.

The Buffalo Bills were in a great draft spot. Trades had given them a pair of first-round picks. They used the second to select Kelly, whose Pennsylvania home was a relatively easy drive from Buffalo. Jim Kelly would be coming home—they thought.

Jim steps into the pocket and throws, just as coach Marv Levy drew it in the playbook.

CHAPTER FOUR

THE
PROS

Kelly's agents were meeting with Bills officials when the call came. A new spring league, the United States Football League, wanted Jim Kelly. It wanted him a lot.

The USFL knew it would have to sign some major talent to be considered a major football league. And everyone in football knew that Jim Kelly more than filled the bill. The check they were waving had no dollar amount on it. Kelly could fill in his own numbers.

The deal was too good to turn down.

Suddenly the Buffalo Bills would have to look for another quarterback, and the USFL's Houston Gamblers were ready to rock and roll with Jim Kelly running their offense.

Houston coach Mouse Davis had invented a new offense that he called "the run-and-shoot." It was a pass-happy offense, with running plays used occasionally, just to keep the defense honest. It was a perfect offense for Jim Kelly.

Between the Gamblers' offense, Kelly's skills, and the weak USFL defenses, Jim and his team went crazy. In two years, Kelly completed 713 of 1,154 passes for an unreal 83 touchdowns. He even ran the ball 113 times for 663 yards and six scores. He had sixteen 300-yard games and three 400-yard efforts. In the 1985 season opener against the Los Angeles Express, he practically drove the numbers experts up the wall. He tossed 54 passes and completed 35 of them for an incredible 574 yards and five TDs. In two years in the USFL, Jim failed to throw a touchdown pass in a game only once.

Jim looks back fondly on his USFL years. "I learned a lot and I enjoyed myself," he says. "I'm just sorry all of my yards and TDs don't count in my NFL stats. The only trouble was that I got pounded almost every time I threw the ball. That's the way the run-and-shoot works. The quarterback gets beaten up. I didn't love that part of it."

Just as suddenly as the USFL started, it ended. Some of the owners wanted to keep playing in the spring; others wanted to move to the fall and challenge the NFL. While all of that was going on, the league went out of business. That left

Jim Kelly without a team—for about an hour-and-a-half.

When the Gamblers tossed their last pass, the Buffalo Bills were ready—and waiting. They quickly agreed to terms with their 1983 first-round draft pick. True, it took until August 19, 1986, to sign him, but the wait was worth it. When Kelly's plane landed in Buffalo, Bills fans, hungry for a championship, lined the route from the airport to the stadium. They had their hero now.

But success didn't come overnight. It almost never does. Before Kelly and the Bills were ready to step to the head of the AFC, they'd have to pay their dues. Some experts questioned whether Kelly was ready to be a winning NFL quarterback. They didn't know whether his USFL numbers meant anything; the NFL would be so much tougher. But from day one, Jim showed the upstate New York crowd that he was the guy to get the job done.

With nearly 220 pounds hanging on his 6'3" frame, Jim was plenty tough. There was never any question about his arm. In the 1986 season opener, he completed 20 of 33 passes for 292 yards and three TDs, one of them a 55-yarder. It wasn't enough. The visiting New York Jets hung on for a 28–24 win. The pattern for the season had been set.

When he had time to pass, Kelly was an All-Pro. For the season, he completed 285 of his 480 passes for 3,593 yards, the second highest total in Bills history. His 22 TD passes included a pair of bombs (84 and 75 yards) to wide receiver Chris Burkett. But too often, 43 times in fact, Jim found himself on his back with the ball still in his hands. Jim Kelly never wanted to be among the league leaders in sacks.

By midseason, head coach Hank Bullough had been shown the door. His replacement was veteran NFL coach Marv Levy. It was the start of a beautiful relationship.

The 1987 season was one of the strangest ever. The Bills hired Bobby Ross, a tremendously successful passing coach, as their new offensive coordinator. It looked like the perfect match for Kelly. Within days, however, Ross took a job as head coach at Georgia Tech. Levy had to find a new coordinator—and fast! He turned to Ted Marchibroda, former NFL quarterback and coach of the Baltimore Colts. Kelly and Marchibroda turned out to be a perfect match.

But the weirdness of '87 didn't end

there. Two weeks into the season (the Bills were 1–1), the NFL players went on strike. Fill-ins wore Bills uniforms for the next three games. Talk about strange. The counterfeit Bills went 1–2, before Kelly and the rest of the NFL players returned.

Jim was in great form. When the Bills blew away the Miami Dolphins on November 29, Buffalo had won four of six games. It was the turnaround Bills fans were waiting for.

In Kelly's 12 games that season, Buffalo went 6–6, a major improvement. Jim set a team record for accuracy (59.7%), completing 250 of 419 passes for 2,798 yards, and threw for 19 TDs. Twice he was voted AFC Offensive Player of the Week. Kelly threw 141 consecutive passes without an interception until the Patriots ended the streak on the next-to-last week of the season.

That's the same week Kelly's streak of 18 straight games with at least one TD pass also ended. Twice that season, against Houston and Miami, Jim rallied his troops to victory in the final minute of the game. That pattern would continue throughout his career.

As the 1988 season opened, Bills fans knew that something special was in the air. For four years, Buffalo had finished at the bottom of the AFC East. It had been eight years since the team's last AFC East championship, but that would change in 1988. Cornelius Bennett, Shane Conlan, and Bruce Smith keyed an improved defense. And Oklahoma State star Thurman Thomas became the running back Kelly needed so badly.

The Bills raced out of the gate, winning 11 of their first 12 games. The city of Buffalo went crazy. With Kelly at the helm, the team won games few expected them to win. In a game at New England, Jim hit on 14 of 18 passes, including 12 in a row, as the Bills rallied for an unbelievable 16–14 victory. Three weeks later, Buffalo trailed the Colts, 17–0, at halftime before Jim pulled the game out of the fire, 34–23.

"You have to believe in Jim," said linebacker Ray Bentley. "No matter how far we're behind, we know that he can bring us back."

The Bills wound up 12–4, winning the AFC East title. Kelly had 269 completions (second best in club history) and hit on 59.5% of his passes, just under his 1987 team mark.

On New Year's Day, 1989, Buffalo beat Houston, 17–10, for its first playoff win in seven years. But with a Super

Bowl ticket and the AFC champion-ship at stake in Cincinnati the following week, Buffalo fell to the Bengals, 21–10.

No matter. The Bills were back. A championship in 1989 was a real possi-bility—until the season actually began. It quickly became evident that no one could beat them — except themselves.

The '89 campaign started brilliantly. The first game was vintage Kelly. Trailing Miami by 24–13 with less than four minutes to go, the Bills came up huge. When Jim ran the ball over from the two-yard line to wrap up a 27–24 victo-ry, the scoreboard clock read 0:00. What a great way to open the year!

A couple of weeks later, Jim was at it again. He outdueled Houston's Warren Moon, with 363 yards and five TDs. His 28-yarder to Andre Reed in overtime gave Buffalo a 47–40 victory. The Bills

It's easier to pass when you can hand off to talented Thurman Thomas on running plays.

were 3–1, and Kelly was in charge.

The following Sunday, the wheels began to come off the wagon. In the third quarter of a 37–14 loss to Indianapolis, Kelly went down with a separated shoulder. He'd be out for at least three weeks. The following day, Jim blew his cool, blaming a young offensive tackle for missing a block and causing his injury. His outcry was a serious mistake. The press jumped all over him. The fans jumped all over him. And his teammates were even angrier. Several of them attacked Jim on TV. It was messy.

The Bills won their next three games with backup Frank Reich at quarterback. But when Jim returned, the team proceeded to lose five of its next seven. Though they wound up 9–7, three games behind their 1988 record, they still won the AFC East and moved on to the play-offs vs. favored Cleveland.

That's when the healing began. Coach Marchibroda designed a brand-new short passing game for Kelly, with Thurman Thomas as the No. 1 receiver. Jim threw for 405 yards and four TDs, but the Bills came up short, just short. With only 14 seconds to go, Jim threw what should have been his fifth TD pass. But Ronnie Harmon, all alone in the corner of the end zone, dropped the ball. On the following play, Kelly was intercepted by Clay Matthews at the one-yard line. It was over. Cleveland won, 34–30, but the Bills had momentum for 1990. The bleeding had stopped.

During the off-season, Jim signed a new six-year contract for big bucks. Meanwhile, the Bills coaches planned carefully for a Super Bowl year.

Since the Kelly-led offense was

always outstanding in the last two minutes of games, why not play the whole game that way? Thus, the Bills' now-famous no-huddle offense was built. Anytime the Bills had the ball, they might score — in a hurry.

In 1990 Jim was up to his old tricks. Against the tough Philadelphia Eagles, he had three TDs and 334 yards. He had four scores in horrible weather against the Phoenix Cardinals. Against the Colts, he hit 28 of 37 for 283 yards and a score. His 14-yarder to Jamie Mueller with only 19 seconds to go produced a 30–27 win against the Jets.

The Bills were practically unstoppable. They wound up the season with a league-high 428 points and a team-record 13 wins. But with the play-offs ready to open, Jim was a question mark. He had torn up his left knee against the

Giants and missed the last two regular-season games. Would he be ready for the postseason?

"I'll be there," said Kelly. And was he ever! In the opener against AFC-rival Miami, Jim threw a 20-yarder to Thurman Thomas, followed by a 40-yarder to Andre Reed. He wound up with 339 yards, three TDs, and a 44–34 victory.

The following week, in the AFC championship game, the Bills put on one of the greatest displays of offense ever. Against the Los Angeles Raiders, Kelly completed 17 of 23 for 300 yards and two TDs. He even picked up a fumble and tossed it into the end zone for a score. Buffalo won the game, 51–3, and a ticket to Super Bowl XXV in Tampa. Jim Kelly had taken the Bills where no Bills team had ever gone before.

Buffalo came into the year's biggest game as a clearcut favorite. Someone forgot to tell the Giants, however. The New York team that plays in New Jersey held the ball for more than 40 of the game's 60 minutes. Jim wasn't up to his usual standard, thanks to the Giants' great defensive pressure. Kelly hit on 18 of 30 for 212 yards but no TDs. Still, it took a missed 47-yard Scott Norwood field goal in the final four seconds to seal the Bills' fate. The Giants won, 20–19, but the Bills would be back.

In 1991 the AFC still couldn't figure out a way to stop Buffalo. On opening day, Kelly threw for a career best 381 yards and two TDs in a 35–31 win against the Dolphins. The next week, he threw for a club-record six TDs and 363 yards to pace a 52–34 victory over Pittsburgh. He had five more scores and a new club-record 392 yards against the Bengals in October for a 35–16 win.

By the end of the season, Jim had re-written the record book with 33 TDs, 3,844 yards, 64.1% accuracy, and 474 completions. Kelly was No. 12 on the roster but No. 1 in the hearts of Bills fans.

Now came the play-offs and the road to Super Bowl XXVI. It wouldn't be easy. Kansas City had beaten the Bills, 33–6, in October. Now the Chiefs were coming to Buffalo for an AFC semifinal rematch. No contest. Jim threw 25- and 53-yard TD strikes to Andre Reed and a 10-yarder to James Lofton. Buffalo rolled up 448 yards and 29 first downs. Final score: 37–14, Buffalo.

The AFC final against Denver figured to be just as easy. It wasn't. The Broncos missed three field goals, and Denver QB John Elway fired a costly interception that linebacker Carlton Bailey returned for a score. Meanwhile, Buffalo could muster only 213 yards, only 104 through the air, and no touchdowns. Somehow Buffalo managed to win, 10–7, to earn a second straight Super Bowl trip.

Kelly and Company should have stayed home. The Washington Redskins battered Jim and his mates, shutting down the Bills for most of the first three quarters. Jim found himself on his back five times, and he threw four interceptions. Washington won, 37–24. The Bills, who arrived in Minneapolis with great hope, went home empty — again.

Back at the Bills hotel after the game, Jim Kelly sat on the edge of his bed and apologized to everyone for his sorry performance. But the team's defeat was hardly his fault. His offensive line was

Even stacked three high, Cleveland defenders can't stop Kelly from throwing deep.

awful, the Bills running game was worse, and Jim's receivers dropped pass after pass, including two sure touchdowns. Still, it was the leader, Jim Kelly, who apologized.

"That's the kind of guy he is," said his old high school coach, Terry Henry, Jim's guest at the big game. "He's an incredibly caring person. A lot of people never get to see that side of Jim. He's close to his old teammates, and there isn't a better family man anywhere."

Actually Jim is among the city's most eligible bachelors. He lives on a winding street in Orchard Park, where the Bills' Rich Stadium is located. His neighbors include some of Buffalo's rich and famous. But none are as famous as he.

Jim's house is typical of the area. It's a large stone and natural wood modern home with a circular driveway. Inside, the furnishings are modern, too. The quarterback's pride and joy is his play-room in the basement, featuring a sports hall of fame. Framed throughout the room are autographed uniforms from some of Kelly's famous friends, including Julius Erving, Boomer Esiason, Terry Bradshaw, Wayne Gretzky, and others. The centerpiece is the uniform, with number 11 sewn on, that Jim wore at East Brady High School.

Although Jim's family live all around the country, they remain the focus of his life. His parents come up from East Brady in their specially equipped RV every time the Bills are at home. Travel is difficult now for Jim's mom, who suffers from emphysema. But she tries to make as many games as she can.

Jim spreads his wealth around the family. He takes his brothers and sistersin-law on vacation every year and invited his father and uncle to join him on a trip to London — with a private tour of Ireland thrown in.

"I love to play Santa Claus," says Jim. "I have more than I ever dreamed I would. I enjoy being able to treat my family the way I have."

Though Jim usually keeps up a tough image, he absolutely melts for kids. "Everything I do for charity is devoted to kids and kids' causes," he says. "I remember when things were tough for us. So I try to make things a little easier for today's kids."

Can Jim lead the Bills to another Super Bowl — and win the famous ring? It's going to be a huge challenge. But, as Terry Henry says, "Jim has accepted every challenge he has ever faced. He'll do it!"

CAREER HIGHLIGHTS

- National semifinalist in Punt, Pass, and Kick contest at age 10.

- Led East Brady (PA) High School to an undefeated football season in his senior year. Months later, paced East Brady basketball team to Pennsylvania state semifinals, averaging 23 points and 20 rebounds per game.

- Led 17–14 victory over Penn State in 1982, which vaulted Miami into top spot in college rankings.

- Won MVP award in the USFL, leading Houston Gamblers to 22 wins in 32 starts over two years.

- As NFL rookie with Buffalo Bills in '86, set a team record with 283 completions.

- Won first Pro Bowl selection in '87, with streak of 141 passes in a row without interception.

- Tied NFL play-off record in '89 with four TD passes against Cleveland Browns.

- Led Buffalo to its first Super Bowl appearance with 44–34 victory over Miami and 51–3 destruction of L.A. Raiders in '90.

- AFC's top-rated quarterback in '91, Kelly hit 64.1% of his passes and threw for 33 TDs, leading Bills to second straight Super Bowl visit.